The Agile Manager's Guide To

CUTTING COSTS

By Jeff Olson

Velocity Business Publishing
Bristol, Vermont USA

For Haley

Copyright © 1997 by Velocity Business Publishing, Inc.
All Rights Reserved
Printed in the United States of America
Library of Congress Catalog Card Number 97-90826
ISBN 0-9659193-3-1
Title page illustration by Elayne Sears
Second printing, August 1999

If you'd like additional copies of this book or a catalog of books in the Agile Manager Series™, please get in touch.

- **Write us:**
  Velocity Business Publishing, Inc.
  15 Main Street
  Bristol, VT 05443 USA

- **Call us:**
  1-888-805-8600 in North America (toll-free)
  1-802-453-6669 from all other countries

- **Fax us:**
  1-802-453-2164

- **E-mail us:**
  action@agilemanager.com

- **Visit our Web site:**
  www.agilemanager.com

The Web site contains much of interest to business people—tips and techniques, business news, links to valuable sites, and instant downloads of titles in the Agile Manager Series.

Contents

Books in the Agile Manager Series™:

Introduction

In good times, even the stingiest managers among us tend toward excess. We buy the latest personal productivity technology, hire more people in anticipation of growth, add a few junkets to our travel plans, and buy items that catch our fancy—like $1,200 ergonomic chairs.

None of these things improves our ability to please customers, so when leaner times come, or sanity returns, we have to cut back.

If you must cut costs, this book will prove invaluable. It spotlights whole pockets of expense you can chop out without sacrificing your ability to serve customers. And it may even help you serve them better.

The book will be even more valuable for those who want to gain a long-term edge by *containing* costs. Among the ways to do that, you'll read, is to set up and optimize business systems that deliver results to customers. These include redesigning products so they cost less to produce, managing inventory better, adhering to strict hiring guidelines, and reengineering key processes.

When you do a good job containing costs, there's less reason to cut in the face of economic decline. You're already running a lean operation focused entirely on customer needs.

This is an idea book. Department or division managers will find it useful to meet their profitability or productivity goals. So will entrepreneurs thirsting for profitability, new managers who need an overview of sound cost containment, and senior executives whose people can't seem to control costs.

Written in a quick-read format, this book summarizes the best ideas, methods, and techniques managers have used for years to cut costs. You can read it in a couple of sittings, then keep it close by for ideas when you need them.

"Watch your costs, and the profits will take care of themselves," said steel magnate Andrew Carnegie a century ago. The best managers don't agonize over the size of their profits or earnings. They know that providing useful products and services, optimizing their systems for the benefit of customers, and keeping a lid on costs is guarantee enough that the market, shareholders, and senior managers will reward their streetsmarts and initiative.

The Philosophy Of Cutting Costs

*"Reducing costs, increasing compensation, or providing
more training are usually not the solutions
to organizational problems."*

RICHARD A. MORAN
IN *NEVER CONFUSE A MEMO WITH REALITY*

Chapter One

Know Your Costs

The Agile Manager read the memo for the fourth time. The lone sentence containing the essence seemed, by now, to be written in bold: "As a result, every department must cut its costs—<u>across the board</u>—by 5 percent through the end of the fiscal year."

He murmured, "How are we going to do that? And why should I have to worry about an 'extraordinary charge' based on something that happened in Asia two years ago?"

But that's reality, old boy, he said to himself. Deal with it. He buzzed Wanda. No answer.

"Steve!" he called to his assistant in the next room.

"Yeah, boss?" said Steve, poking his head in the door.

"Can you find Wanda and have her come in here immediately, please? Pull her out of a meeting if you have to."

"Sure thing." Steve left quickly. He rarely saw his boss this agitated, and the peevish tone of his voice said, "Don't ask what's up."

When Wanda, second-in-command in the product development department, came in, the Agile Manager said, "Here, read this." He gave her a moment. "Can you believe it? Some bonehead VP makes a major mistake and we all have to pay. And you and I run the tightest ship in the organization."

"Well, I just heard the bonehead got canned this morning, if it makes you feel any better."

"It doesn't," said the Agile Manager. "He probably got some lump-sum payment that allows him to lie around on a beach in Bermuda for a couple of months."

"Probably," said Wanda, "but that won't make it any easier for him to get another job." She smiled and said, "Listen, let's make this a game. Sure, we run a lean department. But that doesn't mean there's no fat. And it'll give us an opportunity to look over how we do things. I know it's a cliché, but if we all pull together . . ."

"Cut costs!" bellows the CEO or your immediate boss. Often that exhortation is necessary. Your department or division—or the whole company—has become fat and complacent.

If so, senior managers have, most likely, taken their eyes off the ball. In business, the "ball" is satisfying customers. To do that takes great products or services, and lean, efficient systems for delivering them.

But to err is human. When cash flow is good, we all relax. Sooner or later, however, we pay for our excesses. Sometimes we pay in a matter of months, sometimes in years. But pay we must—by taking a scalpel, and sometimes an ax, to the budget.

Put Cost-cutting in Perspective

Cost-cutting has become a mantra for managers weaned in the late 1980s and 1990s. With so much cost-cutting and down-sizing going on, it's easy for some managers to forget that the purpose of business is to create and keep customers. That's what grows revenues and usually profits. It also hides or eases at least some of the spending sins hidden in the profit-and-loss statement.

By denouncing what they call "denominator managers" in their bestseller *Competing for the Future*, business theorists Gary Hamel and C. K. Prahalad remind us of the real reason for being in business—to create customers.

Here's what they mean by that phrase: Top managers succeed

by improving their return on investment (ROI). The numerator in the equation is net income, and the denominator can be investment, capital, net assets, or, in service firms, headcount. To improve ROI, you can raise the figure in the numerator or lower the figure in the denominator.

It's easier to lower the bottom figure, so that's what most managers do. They chop away hundreds of costly people, sell assets, and starve R&D. Voilà! Improved ROI. (But for how long?)

In the long term, it's much harder to improve net income. That means going beyond one-time cost-cutting events and raising revenues—by understanding customers better, entering or creating new markets, or investing in plant, people, and equipment.

Best Tip

Don't let a passion for cost-cutting snuff out innovation.

Hamel and Prahalad are right on the money. And that's why Richard Moran, in this section's epigraph, states that cost-cutting is "usually not the [solution] to organizational problems."

While it's desperately important to contain costs (and cut them drastically when we've grown complacent), it's more important to focus on satisfying customers by giving them what they want at the lowest cost possible. Don't let a passion for cost-cutting snuff out innovation. You're in business to serve customers, not to squeeze costs to zero.

Good Cost Containment Takes Foresight

Satisfying customers at low cost is a matter of foresight, effective planning, optimizing systems and processes continually, and careful budgeting. It is more a matter of cost *containment* than cost-cutting.

At a company I once worked at, sales tripled while headcount remained the same. That's a phenomenon that doesn't happen by accident. The manager in charge of systems worked daily at optimizing them, often by prudent investment in information technology, but also by redesigning work processes often. The tinkering paid off—not only for the company, but also for customers: The wizardry our operations manager practiced ensured that prices remained stable while the quality of service improved.

Indiscriminate Cost-cutting Is Dangerous

Long-term cost containment is not a matter of carving out costs indiscriminately—especially the kind of cost-cutting that damages the company's muscle and bone.

As many observers have pointed out, restructurings designed to do one thing only—like get rid of 1,125 people—often end up raising costs rather than lowering them.

How can that be? The knife-wielders think only about getting rid of people and selling assets, and not about eliminating work or optimizing work flow. Thus, after downsizings, temporary workers are brought in, consultants are used more often, work once done in-house is outsourced, and those left on the staff are demoralized, overworked, and inefficient.

Know the Different Costs

Before you begin cutting costs, then, you must be aware of which are productive, and which are either wasteful or could be eliminated without harming the company.

Peter Drucker, as usual, offers the most useful analysis of costs. He reminds us first that costs are best viewed as expenses that get results. Such expenses, like spending on technology or research, are not only money well spent. They are necessary.

Drucker categorizes costs, in part, this way:

Productive costs: These costs provide value to the customer. They include selling, manufacturing, and research costs.

Support costs: These include accounting, trucking, order fulfillment, etc. Such costs, though necessary, usually don't benefit customers. Cut them to the bone while maintaining acceptable levels of service.

Waste: Waste produces no value whatsoever. Wasteful items include rich travel budgets or lavish office space. Root out waste diligently.

Before you cut costs, then, it's essential that you know exactly what you are doing. You cut productive costs—like reducing the capital-investment budget—at your peril. And while it's not always easy to cut necessary support costs, you can shop around for better prices or redesign systems to eliminate the need for them.

Best Tip

Look at "good" costs as expenses that get results. Banish costs that produce no value at all.

Don't Target the Trivial

Superficial cost-cutting, while probably not fatal, can be annoying. Some companies cut costs by skimping on travel expenses for necessary trips, or by making it hard to get a few extra pens. Such efforts rarely have the desired effect and instead demoralize people.

It makes much more sense to rethink how you operate—and whether you need to do certain kinds of work at all. Cutting out whole, unnecessary operations saves a lot more money than forcing people to fly from Chicago to Los Angeles by way of Houston to save a few bucks.

Consider Yourself an Outsourcer

Some very smart senior managers contain costs and grow their core businesses at the same time by subcontracting out whole operations. These may be support services like benefits planning, logistics, or information technology. Some companies go even farther by subcontracting out design and manufacturing. (Cellular phone maker Nokia not only does both those things but outsources sales as well.)

As chapter seven will show, outsourcing done poorly can wreck a business. Done well, it can put it on the top tier among its competitors.

But for now, forget about whether it's done well or badly. The important thing is that it's being done more all the time. And that means your department or division faces competition from anyone outside the company that can do what you do better or more efficiently (or both).

Start thinking of the area you control as a stand-alone business that must do what any business must—satisfy customers. The only difference is that your customers may be inside the firm.

Seeing yourself as CEO of your own business will help you understand the need to watch expenses, plan long-term strategies to contain costs, and improve productivity.

Even if your department is under no threat from outsourcers, operating this way can spotlight it—and you—favorably.

In General . . .

A simple benchmark exists for evaluating a cost: Does it serve the customer?

"Good" costs support the product or service that gets you a customer. "Bad" costs—those that can be reduced or removed altogether—don't.

The rest of this book will help you identify both kinds of costs and what to do about them.

The Agile Manager's Checklist

✔ Remember: In the long-term, it's more important to raise revenues than to cut costs.
✔ Think more in terms of cost containment than cost-cutting.
✔ Know the kinds of costs:
  ■ Productive costs, which provide value to customers;
  ■ Support costs, necessary but of no value to customers;
  ■ Waste.

Everyday Cost-Cutting

"Avoid waterfalls in the lobby."

JIM SCHELL
IN *SMALL-BUSINESS MANAGEMENT GUIDE*

Chapter Two

Eliminate Waste

"Do we have to cut costs directly," asked William, "or can we sell stuff and put long-term cost-saving programs into place, too? I mean you could, after all, achieve the goal today by firing two or three of us."

"I'm not gonna do that, Willie," said the Agile Manager. "Here's how I'm going to interpret that memo: At the end of the fiscal year, nine months from now, I'd better not have spent more than my budget—minus 5 percent. If I go over that, I'm assuming you'll find my head on a pole in the courtyard."

"That serious, huh?" asked William.

"Yes, sir. But we have some leeway, and we can get through this without laying anyone off. The long-term stuff you mentioned sounds good—if you can call nine months long term. What have you got in mind?"

"Well, first of all, that storage closet on the second floor has some old equipment I'm sure we can sell. There's a market for old analyzers and testers—mainly electronics hobbyists, but also collectors. I have no idea what they are worth, but I can find out."

"Go ahead," said the Agile Manager. "What else?"

"I may be about to offend you—"

"Don't hold back," said the Agile Manager stoically.

"OK . . . that consultant you hired to scout new product ideas is a chump. He's one of those guys who makes you think he's really up on things—he knows everyone, knows all the buzzwords—but I haven't seen a single good idea in two months now." The Agile Manager laughed, his eyebrows twitching.

"You're the third person to tell me that today. He's history. Now, what about those long-term cost-cutting programs?"

If you need to cut costs now, this chapter is for you.

Concentrate Your Efforts

When you begin to think of cutting waste, keep in mind the 80/20 rule. Also known as Pareto's Law, or the rule of the trivial many and significant few, it says that 20 percent of the activities account for 80 percent of the results.

That means that about 80 percent of your costs come from 20 percent of your activities. Or 80 percent of the waste comes from 20 percent of your expense categories.

It thus pays to scan your budgets and financial statements to identify the few categories that produce the greatest expense. These may include areas of waste, like too-lavish entertainment budgets or employee benefits, expenditures for office and ware-house space, or the maintenance costs on outdated equipment. Sometimes the big culprit is too many people, so we've devoted a whole chapter to that (chapter eight).

Cut These Items

Here's a laundry list of likely candidates for the chopping (or auction) block:

Unneeded assets. Walk around the office or factory and iden-tify underutilized, inefficient, or useless items. Inspect, carefully, storage rooms and warehouses. Also, don't forget that even use-less items carry a cost—they take up space and may be hazard-ous. Investigate out-of-the-way corners or rooms filled with junk and deal with them.

Sometimes unneeded items are quite large. Al Dunlap, when

named CEO of Scott Paper, wasted no time in selling off the company's three-building, 750,000-square-foot headquarters complex for $39 million. A slimmed-down management team fit comfortably into 30,000 square feet.

Slow-moving inventories. It's hard, psychologically, to sell off, at fire-sale prices, inventory that cost you so much to build up. But too-high inventories cost you in insurance expenses, space used, and paperwork and personnel. On top of that, standard accounting practice prevents you from expensing inventory until it's sold. All in all, slow-moving inventory consumes cash. If you're in doubt about that, have your numbers man or woman analyze your inventory's cost. That might wake you up.

Consider your company or department a bank. The money is hidden not in a vault but in unneeded assets.

Consultants. Some companies never use consultants. They do just fine—just ask Wal-Mart. And ask yourself: Are you using a consultant because you're afraid to take a stand?

Companies often use big name consultants to ensure they are keeping up with competitors' "best practices." But good companies often become a benchmark for others through independent thinking and initiative.

Company cars. Sure, your salespeople need them. But are they just perks for the non-salespeople who have them? Think of the costs beyond paying for the car: maintenance, insurance, and record-keeping (both for the company and the executive). Best advice: Pay key people more and let them buy and maintain their own vehicles.

Travel budget. Do executives get anywhere faster flying first or business class? Must they stay at the Peninsula when the Marriott would do? Should they eat at the city's best French restaurant instead of the hotel's dining room? Let them live high on their own time if they want to (they won't, except rarely).

Don't skimp on travel—you want people refreshed and productive—but don't forget: The mattress in a $300-a-night room is just as comfortable to a tired manager as the one in an $89 room.

A simple rule of thumb: Ask people to spend money as if it were their own. It'll be obvious when they don't.

Entertainment. Some people, those in high-level sales for instance, really do require a substantial entertainment budget. Taking a client to the best restaurant in town can pay off. But question most such expenses, especially on-going cash drainers like club memberships.

Some people will argue strenuously that it's very important for them to be seen at the club, eat out often with clients, go to functions, and travel to resorts for conventions. They may have good reason. But some people simply like to socialize in a nice atmosphere, and they've convinced themselves (and you) that it's necessary.

Lawyers. Some companies get lawyers involved in everything "just to be safe." Yes, have lawyers draw up contracts and handle lawsuits. But must they get involved in new product planning (the liability angle) and every little personnel problem? You decide, but be aware that some companies do just fine by keeping lawyers at arm's length.

Industry or association dues. Money for these can be well spent. But at least estimate what you get for what you pay.

Too much space. It's no wonder that large companies are selling off office buildings and settling in smaller surroundings. You can save a lot of money. Sears, for example, wisely sold its headquarters, the tallest building in Chicago, and moved to suburban Hoffman Estates, Illinois. In that city, few buildings top six or eight stories.

Two good reasons for skimping on space: First, the home-office revolution is real and has barely begun. There will be less and less need for central, and spacious, office locations. Second, files in some offices take up as much as 30 percent of floor space.

With technology breakthroughs, paper storage of information is fast becoming unnecessary. In short, space that seems inadequate today may be perfectly adequate tomorrow—with even more people on the staff.

Warehouse space is usually used more intelligently than office space, but not always. Analyze its use as well. Companies often find they can save a bundle by consolidating warehouses, and without harming customer service.

Be wary of increasing office floor space. Home workers and digital files may one day give back space now in use.

Upgrade your office's mechanical systems. I once had an office with electric heat in a cold climate. I can't think of a bigger waste of money.

Shop around for essential supplies. Thank goodness for warehouse supply stores like Costco. They've shown us that we all have overpaid for supplies for years.

Shop around for telephone services. I hate to suggest that anyone get involved in buying telephone services—it's extremely difficult to get a straight answer about anything—but it's an area ripe for cost savings. My company recently halved its daytime long-distance charges by changing providers.

Drop marginal customers. To some this is heresy. But never forget the 80/20 rule: 20 percent of your customers account for 80 percent of your sales or profits. Those at the other end of the spectrum cost you dearly, either because they order little for the attention you give them, or because they are impossible to please.

Dump them, and you win in a variety of ways: Fewer people needed to sell to and service customers, less overhead, less warehouse space, less in the way of advertising or printing costs, etc.

Keep the marginal customers who may grow into big customers one day. You'll know who they are.

Insurance deductibles. Raising deductibles for insurance saves you a lot of money over the long haul. And you can bet that your insurance company's quotes are for low deductibles unless you request otherwise.

Don't Cut in These Areas

Sometimes—especially when your back is against the wall— you'll be tempted to cut costs in areas that could harm you:

Salaries, benefits, or bonuses or gifts expected. Once you give in these areas, you'd better not take away—except under extreme duress. Today's generosity is tomorrow's entitlement. It's best to be less generous today if your capacity to be generous next year is in doubt.

Best **T**ip
Don't cut salaries, benefits, or perks, except under extreme duress.

Commissions, royalties, etc. Don't cut the money you pay outsiders who send business your way or otherwise aid your operations. If you do, you'll create an instant band of enemies. Airlines regularly squeeze travel agents, for instance, but at an incalculable cost in good will.

Marketing. Never cut your sales and marketing budget without great forethought. One false move here and the whole game might be over.

Your budget for productive assets. A man I know works for a publisher of industry magazines. He, and all the other writers and editors, still work on old IBM PCs that lack hard drives. The cost in productivity to this company is enormous. Besides the daily inefficiency of working on outdated computers, good people don't stick around long. Spend thoughtfully but liberally on anything that makes your people more productive.

Anything that helps maintain steady production. Give people all the tools and supplies they need to be productive. If they must travel, make sure they have enough money available to remain happy and refreshed. If they must use a car, keep it clean and well maintained. If the office is dingy, paint it and lay new carpet. The psychological boost will cover your costs.

Eliminate Wastes of Time

It's been estimated that people are productive only half the time they spend at work. The other half is spent on personal business, socializing, needless meetings, unnecessary travel, and useless activities.

Managers in the best-run companies stay on top of their people to produce. They get rid of talkers, for example, or those who love a good junket.

Meetings are among the biggest time-wasters. Before you attend any meeting, insist on knowing its purpose (assuming you have enough clout). Ask for a written agenda in advance and the minutes afterward. Act on the outcome and do your best to ensure others do, too.

Good managers also keep their people focused on productive tasks—not reports that never get read, memos "for the file," or projects that don't have a chance of getting approved. And they protect their people as best they can from meddling managers with an agenda counter to the team's purpose.

Finally, good managers keep people on time. Workers arrive on time, for instance, and meetings start and end on time.

The Agile Manager's Checklist

✔ You'll find 80 percent of the waste in 20 percent of the budget categories.
✔ Consider dropping marginal customers.
✔ Weed out wastes of time, including useless meetings and pointless reports or memos.

Chapter Three

Contain Those Costs

"Here's another one," said Chuck, an accountant from head-quarters on loan for a few days to the product-development department. "Your account called 'Prototypes' is a real spike."

"That's an important account," said the Agile Manager. "We need to spend to build prototypes. If we skimp there, they don't tell us what we need to know about feasibility."

"I'm not saying it's not important," said Chuck. "But it towers over other accounts I would've guessed would be in the same range, like Design Costs. And at the rate you're going, you'll be way over budget at the end of the fiscal year."

"Hmm," said the Agile Manager, puzzled. "It often comes in over budget, but I've learned to compensate for it by balancing that account with a couple of others in which we usually spend less. I'll look into it."

Chuck stared at him, wondering how he prepared his budgets. Maybe I should drop a hint, he thought. "You know, I could take a few hours and go over with you how to prepare accurate budgets. It's a great place to set some productivity targets, too . . ."

*　　　*　　　*

"You do what?" asked the Agile Manager.

"Just what I said," said Phil. "We always throw focus groups into that account. And they're expensive—you gotta pay 'em, feed 'em lunch, give 'em a gift—"

"I know all that. But why charge it to Prototypes?"

"That's what Len used to do before me. What account would you charge it to?"

The Agile Manager fumbled through his mind looking for the right account title, but nothing seemed to fit.

Phil continued. "And that's not all. That account is a dumping ground for miscellaneous items. We sometimes put business lunches in there—only when they relate to development, of course."

"Thanks," said the Agile Manager abruptly. He headed out the door.

Focus groups, he fumed as he charged down the hallway. I never trust them, yet marketing always insists on them. If I find we've been shouldering the costs for these by ourselves, I'll—

He suddenly had a distressing thought: Do Wanda and I really run a tight ship? If I'd been doing my job, shouldn't I have known about this sooner? And that guy Chuck wondering why I don't build productivity improvement into my numbers like some other managers . . .

Cost-cutting is what you do when you've been asleep at the wheel for a while. Cost containing is what good managers do all the time.

Measure and Track Productivity

There is one overarching technique to contain costs: Do more each year with the same or fewer resources. In other words, improve productivity. It's a challenging game.

Setting improvement goals is easy. Succeeding is much harder. It ultimately depends on your skills and resourcefulness, and your willingness to invest, innovate, or empower the people who work for you.

Blue-collar productivity. To play the game, set a productivity-improvement target, like 4 percent a year. Then come up with a measure. For those in a factory setting, or those who produce anything physical, this may be easy. One easy measure of productivity is units produced per man-hour. If your group produces 16,500 widgets per 2000 man hours, for example, that's 16,500/2000 or 8.25/hour. To improve productivity 4 percent gives you a target of 8.58/hour. Multiplying 8.58 by 2000 gives you your new yearly total: 17,160.

Best Tip

Improving productivity ensures you are adding to the bottom line. It'll increase your skills and ability to get things done.

How are you going to pump out those extra 660 widgets? New equipment? Better work practices or improved process flow? Judicious hiring or firing? Coming up with a mix of initiatives to improve output is your job as a manager.

White-collar productivity. Four percent is a meager improvement in most manufacturing settings. A new machine or process can sometimes improve productivity 10 percent or more.

But 4 percent in the service or white-collar sector is, for various reasons, harder. Peter Drucker, in condemning the lack of productivity growth in the service sector, maintains that we need smart people to analyze white-collar work practices much as Frederick Taylor did for manufacturing work a century ago.

Coming up with an adequate productivity measure for service work is also a challenge. An easy, companywide measure is sales or profit per employee, or sales or profit divided by total payroll. Another, especially if you're in a support-service cost center, is costs per employee.

What if you are part of a support service whose budget is under the control of someone else? There's still a formula for you. If you're in charge of a team of typists at a law office, for example, try documents processed per day. Or better yet, words per day. (That's easy to calculate with computers.)

Or say you run a team of computer technicians. Chart successful calls per person per day or week. You could also set goals for doing routine tasks faster. A goal like that compels you to analyze how work gets done and how the process or practice could be improved. That's a valuable use of your time.

Whatever you track, keep this in mind: Don't measure your busyness alone, like transactions processed, unless speed equals value. Make sure your measure somehow takes into account the quality or value you provide.

It would be almost useless for human resources people, for example, to track the number of people they place in jobs. By that measure, the worse job they did getting the right person in the right job, the better they'd look thanks to high turnover. By also measuring the length of tenure in the job, they can measure how well they did the job in the first place.

Value added. Another useful method to measure productivity is value added. It is simple to understand, but it requires that you have access to cost figures.

First, take the value (in dollars) of either the goods or services your operation produces. Then subtract the costs of materials used in the operation. The remainder is the value added, in dollars, by those working in your operation.

Then take the value added and divide by either the number of people involved, by hours worked, or by total payroll. Aim to raise the figure.

Track the trend over time. Productivity measures are useful only if you watch them over time. Collect data daily or weekly, monthly, and yearly. Make sure you track pertinent measures, and keep them consistent from one period to the next. Don't, in other words, change your definition of "transaction" and then

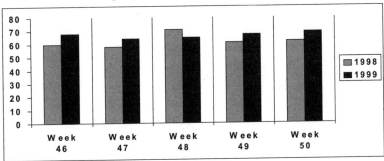

Sample productivity chart showing transactions per week

continue to measure it against previous data.

And use a charting program to illustrate trends graphically. To get your people involved in the game, post these charts. It can be both fun and motivating to beat last month's totals.

Deal with Cost Spikes

The 80/20 rule applies to small operations as well whole companies. That means 80 percent of your costs will come from 20 percent of the activities. Identify the cost spikes within your reach and see if you can lower them.

Imagine you are in charge of accounts receivable for your company. The daily work of the department is to process checks, match invoices, and do a little accounting.

One activity probably sticks out like a sore thumb: Collecting overdue accounts. The department and company pay a cost when customers treat you like a bank that offers no-interest loans. On top of that, you pay by sending repeated dunning notices and spending time on the telephone with the worst offenders.

Maybe you can figure out an innovative way to deal with overdue accounts. A starting point is to measure your collection period. To do that, divide your accounts receivable by average daily credit sales. The result is the collection period.

Best Tip

Don't measure speed or quantity of transactions unless either provides value for customers.

For example, if your receivables total $119,000, and you sell an average of $4,000 worth of goods and services on credit each day, your collection period is 119,000/4,000 or 29.78 days. This figure is great if you're in the book-publishing business, but it's a disaster if you're in the wholesale grocery business.

If the number results in high carrying costs, whittle it down. Maybe a few early, well-timed calls will do the trick. Perhaps having a form letter from your lawyer on hand is the answer.

Maybe you could speed things up by offering a discount for payment in ten days.

Contain Program/Committee Costs

Costs proliferate like weeds. And they often hide in well-meaning programs or activities.

Say you want to put together a team of people to investigate and report on industry best practices. Good idea, but set a time limit on the team's activities—like three months. If it is marvelously productive and returns usable cost-saving ideas, extend the mandate.

*B*est *T*ip
Give people deadlines for every task or project. Help them meet the deadlines by checking in often.

Otherwise, make sure the committee dies an early death. Similarly, watch out for do-gooder committees on things like office recycling or internship programs. Without sunset dates, they become permanent parts of the organization—without anyone ever stopping to think if it's a good idea to add such costs or not.

Training

Good training is an excellent way to contain costs. But the fact is that many companies practice "sink or swim" management at a great cost to the organization. Spend liberally to teach people to do their jobs better. It pays in the long run.

A woman who works in order entry for a distribution company told me a telling story recently. The company switched from a DOS-based database system to a Windows interface. Everyone got one hour of training beforehand. To veteran computer users, this may seem adequate. But few of the people had computers at home or used their work computers for reasons beyond order entry. The jump from DOS to Windows was big.

The result of this inadequate training? The customer service department, in crisis, was forced to shut down for almost four hours one busy afternoon for emergency training.

Be sure to train for specific tasks. There's no proof that team-building exercises like white-water canoeing or ropes courses have any long-term, positive effect.

Create Electronic Links to Customers and Vendors

Peter Solvik, senior vice president and chief information officer at network products-maker Cisco Systems, reports that Cisco saves $200 each time a customer *doesn't* call its support center. Where do customers with problems get solutions? On the company's World Wide Web site, *www.cisco.com*. Each month, tens of thousands of customers log on to get answers to questions. Solvik expects savings of $75 million over a year.

Keep People on Track

Getting the area you're in charge of organized and keeping it that way is perhaps your greatest cost container. Give people deadlines for everything, then hold them to those deadlines. When you miss deadlines, costs mount.

My father, a successful industrial building contractor, pays close attention to scheduling. It's a key to his success.

He begins each construction job by creating a broad schedule with a handful of milestones.

That schedule is easy to produce before a shovel breaks ground. To stay on schedule, however, takes extreme diligence. He or his managers hold weekly meetings with job superintendents called the "Two-Week Look-Ahead." Managers and superintendents see what needs to be done in the next fourteen days, and they come up with a strict timetable that ensures everything gets done.

Note that the Two-Week Look-Ahead meeting occurs weekly. That means managers can make sure that what was supposed to happen the previous week actually happened. They can hold the job superintendent's feet to the fire if need be, or stay on top of subcontractors who are tardy in completing tasks.

Whatever your business, set aside time weekly, if not daily, to ensure you are meeting your schedule.

Prevent Downtime

Most managers wait for a machine to fail, then call a technician. It's a small, occasional cost, they figure, not thinking about the cost of time when people wait around for a machine to be repaired.

If something as mundane as a fax machine fails, for instance, you can expect a backup of users as soon as it is running again. And that also ties up a phone line for those who may want to fax in.

Take an idea from forward-thinking manufacturers: Institute a program of preventive maintenance and rebuilding. Such a program isn't about lubricating here and dusting off there. Repair people may install whole new switches or subassemblies on a machine before the old ones blow. Preventive maintenance is done during off-hours, so it doesn't disrupt operations.

Roy Harmon, a factory productivity expert for Andersen Consulting, suggests having the machine's main user maintain it. It's a way to involve and empower a worker, for one thing. For another, who knows the machine better than someone who uses it all day? (Union work rules may get in the way on the factory floor, but they shouldn't be a problem in the office.)

The Agile Manager's Checklist

✔ Find a way to measure productivity year in and year out.
✔ Uncover the largest areas of expense and systematically whittle them down.
✔ Train to prevent costly rework.
✔ Schedule work wisely and help people meet deadlines. It's a key to big-time success.

Chapter Four

Simplify Your Product/Service Offerings

"But we have three teams of product developers here," said Manuel. "And you're asking us to coordinate better, which would mean a whole new layer of meetings. Then we'd get nothing done." Manuel narrowed his eyes.

The Agile Manager had always encouraged his people to be forthright and to think independently. His managerial philosophy, in times like these, was trying. He had to fight back the urge to tell Manuel to shut up, and then give him orders. "Manuel, first of all, we have a problem—together. We have to cut costs. Your attitude doesn't help. All you're saying to me is, 'I'm busy. Get out of my face.' Right?" The Agile Manager forced a chuckle.

"Well . . . I guess so," Manuel answered. "I'm sorry. But you don't really want this to be my problem, right? My problem is to get the 2600B to manufacturing by July 1."

"I'm just trying to figure out where we can make some changes and save a little money. And I need your help. So, to repeat myself, I asked why every product has different-sized screws, some of them only a few millimeters different. Do you know?"

"Yes. It's because project teams focus on their products alone. Which is good, I think. I don't really want to know what Anita's *doing with the 1800. It would distract me and the others."*

"Well, at the very least, I'm going to ask you all for greater coordination on components. It wouldn't add a 'new layer' of meetings and, besides, it's important. A quick calculation tells me that manufacturing could save somewhere in the range of $25,000 each year if we used the same-sized screws on our top three products. Then there's brackets and other fasteners . . ."

You can cut and contain costs by eliminating products and simplifying the design, manufacturing, and transporting of those that remain. Service companies can do the same if they think of the individual services they perform as products.

Cut the Number of Products You Offer

Cutting the number of products you offer may be the smartest thing you can do. Many cost-cutting manufacturers, for instance, report that product lines are sometimes made up of needless variations on core products, custom jobs for specific customers later rolled out to the broad market, and unprofitable items kept in production to gratify their executive sponsors.

Best Tip

You can cut products and boost profitability at the same time.

Here's what else you cut when you drop a product: costs in design and manufacturing, marketing, warehousing, purchasing, administrative support, and other hidden costs.

Which Products to Cut

Naturally, Pareto's Law prevails among your product offerings. It may not be the classic 80/20 split, but it could be close.

"Chainsaw" Al Dunlap uses profitably a rule of thumb he calls the "Rule of 55." The rule says 50 percent of your products produce only 5 percent of the revenues and profits. That knowledge gives him a strong incentive to cut products. While at Scott

Paper, Dunlap reduced the number of products by five hundred—and increased the market value of the company by $6.5 billion.

Further evidence? A McKinsey & Company study in Germany showed that the most successful manufacturing companies had two products for every 100 million deutsche marks in sales. Less successful companies had nine products per 100 million in sales.

Best Tip

Divide revenues by the number of products you offer. Compare the figure to others in the industry.

Analyze the sales of each product carefully. Identify the 20 to 50 percent that account for most of the revenue, and consider dumping the rest. Cutting products is never easy—especially if the list of cuts includes pet projects of senior managers—but it must be done.

It's likely that many of those you can cut are variations on good-selling core products. You—or somebody—went after a niche that didn't pan out, and then forgot to scale back.

You also may have some products that sell well but aren't worth the cost of making them. They are complicated or difficult to make, leaving profit margins small.

Simplify Products

Once you've cut out unprofitable products, think deeply about how you design and make those that remain. This list will give you some ideas for containing costs:

1. Simplify designs. Reduce the number of components in a product. If possible, make those that remain do double duty as components in other products. Use the same fan housing, for example, in any product that needs one.

2. Use less material overall. The trend toward miniaturization has many cost-saving ramifications: fewer raw materials used, smaller packing boxes and less packing material needed, smaller warehouse space needed, and reduced shipping costs.

3. Design for manufacturability. In world-class outfits, designers make production as easy as they can. They think hard about such things as set-up and changeover times, and how to design in a way that permits custom runs of a product in small batches. To achieve success, they work closely with manufacturing people.

4. Use the same fasteners (and other basic items) across product lines. Roy Harmon, Andersen Consulting's productivity expert, reports that companies can save a bundle just by using screws and bolts of the same size in all their products. Design is simpler, and they get a better price on components.

5. Buy subassemblies from others. Computer makers buy power supplies, hard drives, and so on from subcontractors. Why should they design and make their own subassemblies when others can do it better and cheaper? If other companies make quality subassemblies more efficiently than you can, buy them.

Be careful, however, that you don't subcontract out a key part that gives you a competitive advantage. You may end up teaching a vendor how to compete with you.

6. Use cheaper materials. Changing from a metal housing to a molded-plastic housing, for example, may save you money without sacrificing quality.

7. Standardize packaging. If every product needs its own custom die-cut boxes, watch out. This is not an incidental expense. If you standardize package designs, and the packing containers they require, you can save in ways that may not be obvious.

For example, imagine packing an order on a pallet with cartons all the same size. Now imagine packing that pallet with different-sized boxes. The process won't be nearly as efficient and will take more space.

8. Eliminate quality control. Your goal should be to produce products of acceptable quality without a team of checkers poring over them. Inspectors are costly, they slow things down, and they let others in the process relax a bit. After all, there's always someone downstream to take care of the mistakes.

Have a designated quality supervisor teach everyone to do their own quality checks, and make sure everyone, including you, understands all of a job's quality requirements. Finally, it helps to have a motivated workforce that cares about the quality of whatever it makes. Ensuring that is up to you.

Service providers: Offer package prices on set services. Consumers like to know what they're getting at what cost.

These eight ideas, by themselves, may all seem laughably obvious to you. But a company often has a number of design and engineering teams working on a variety of products. Each is focused in its own sphere, solving problems it considers unique. They are not.

All it takes is a little poking around by a person with enough clout to get people to come together on design fundamentals and a list of standard components.

Eliminate or Simplify Services Offered

Just as you can eliminate or simplify product offerings, you can do the same in services. Here are a few creative examples to get you thinking:

- A fast-food joint offers a special meal with fixed items— hamburger, fries, and a soft drink. It's easier to take and enter an order, easier to prepare, and easier for the customer to remember. Everyone saves time.

- An Internet service provider went from offering about five different pricing plans to a single, flat fee. It no doubt saved lots of administrative time in doing so.

- A construction company builds high-end homes based on five classic designs. Standardizing designs saves everyone money—no need for an architect, for one thing, and the builder gets faster at putting the houses together with less waste.

- A huge Internet "backbone" provider began to offer accounts to individual users in addition to its main customer base—large companies. It got so bogged down in handling customer inquiries and problems that it got out of the business in less than a year.

- A store changed its format and becomes a "dollar store." Everything in it costs a dollar. Easy to ring up sales, zero confusion on the part of buyers.

- A fancy restaurant opened up with a lengthy menu. It soon cut back to a one-page menu, with no apparent loss of business.

- A law office has a series of "package prices" for services—divorce, will, mediation, and so on. These prices funnel clients into standard solutions at a reduced cost. It also relieves the client from worrying about how much the service is going to cost.

- Another law office simplifies its service by limiting its "products" to one. It specializes in personal-injury cases only.

- As any sales person knows, a confused mind always says "no." Offer people only a few services to choose from so they don't get confused. The ultimate? One price for one basic service—like H&R Block tax-preparation service.

The Agile Manager's Checklist

✔ Cut marginal products or services.
✔ Simplify product designs so they use fewer materials and are easier to manufacture.
✔ Outsource the manufacturing of subassemblies—except for those that give you an advantage.
✔ Teach line workers to do their own quality control.

Chapter Five

Increase Velocity

"You're joking," said Todd from Advance Arrow Electronics. "You guys have been the tightest of the tight. It's like I need to give you my fingerprints every time I visit."

Wanda said, "I know. But that's changing. You see, we all have to cut our budgets due to some fiasco in South America or Asia or someplace. It's really shaking things up around here. In a way, it's been healthy. Like someone opened a window and started to let new ideas in."

"It sounds like it. Anyway, theoretically I'd love to 'partner' with you. But tell me what it means."

"I'm not sure what it'll mean in the end. But I'm pushing for getting real close to vendors we trust. And—fingerprints or not—you and one or two other companies are at the top of the list." Wanda gave him a quick smile. "What I hope this means," she continued, "is that you would be in on product development with us from the start. It would put some of the burden on you, because we'd expect you to do some design work and maybe some minor R&D, be here for frequent meetings, and eventually butt heads with our logistics people to institute some kind of just-in-time delivery of components. The payoff for us is we develop products faster and, *we hope, better. Also, you share a little bit of the risk. But there's a payoff for you, too: You get all the work. No putting specs out to bid."*

"Wow," said Todd. "It's like we're getting married or something."

"Maybe, but we'll start out slow. We'll try it for a few products and see where it leads. What do you think?"

"Sign me up," said Todd.

"Great! We're having a meeting here next Thursday, and . . ."

Speed up.

As long as you're not working in a disorganized frenzy, speed is a wonderful way to keep costs at bay and increase productivity—and profitability.

How Speed Improves Profits

The faster your profitable company turns over capital, the more total profit it amasses.

Let's look at how cash cycles through a company. You take cash on hand, for instance, and make or buy inventory. As that inventory sells, it turns into accounts receivable. The receivables eventually turn back into cash, and you pay off your expenses. If you've priced your products appropriately, you've made a profit.

The faster you travel through this cycle, the bigger the total profit by year end. That's why it can make sense to lower your price—and hence profit margin—on a product. Increased sales turns over capital faster, which results in a larger profit by year end.

Note that increasing sales isn't the only way to turn over capital faster. When you increase the speed of getting new products to market, you not only save money that can be employed elsewhere, but you turn cash into inventory faster.

You can also speed up inventory turnover by keeping inventories smaller. And reducing the accounts receivable collection time means you get your cash faster. The faster you get cash, the faster you can invest in more cash-producing products.

Speed, in short, keeps costs down (time is money) and helps you use your capital most productively.

Where to Speed Up

This list will focus your speed-up efforts. You can find whole books on many of the topics listed. If you want to make progress in areas like just-in-time inventory replenishment or product development, read one of them or hire a consultant. (I'd start with the book.)

Speed up:

Product development. Use new-product teams that include people from all functions—engineering, design, marketing, accounting, and manufacturing. Also, include people from vendor firms.

> **Best Tip**
>
> To keep a project on track, freeze specifications by a certain date. Otherwise, deadlines will creep forward.

Team members should do their work concurrently. You'll expend more effort coordinating people, but it's worth the time saved. Other things to keep in mind:

- Freeze the product's specifications by a certain date, otherwise deadlines creep forward at an alarming rate.
- Set challenging deadlines. They energize people.
- Give new-product team members the clout to get resources or support quickly. They are doing important work.
- Look outside the company for solutions. Maybe a vendor can design, test, make, and supply a key part.
- Investigate design plans for other products you've created. Designs may be recyclable.

Decision making. Many feel Internet software companies are moving faster than companies ever have. One reason: They have an easily accessible, non-capital intensive testing ground for their products.

Web browser company Netscape, fastest of the fast, employs

something it calls "surround sound" management. When an issue comes up—even important ones having to do with pricing or a product's features—they immediately round up all key people and make a decision in a half hour or less.

Netscape can move this fast because its people are more plugged into the market for its products than employees in other industries. And a non-hierarchical, "go for it" atmosphere encourages fast decisions. There's a lesson here for all of us.

Inventory turnover. Institute some kind of just-in-time inventory system (both coming and going) so you don't sit on components or—heaven forbid—finished goods any longer than you must. Once esoteric, JIT systems are more and more common as success stories circulate. (Contrary to popular belief, JIT isn't a Japanese idea—Henry Ford banished warehouses at his River Rouge plant before 1920.)

More tips:

- Pareto again: You'll spend most of your money on just a few component parts. Order them in bulk and have them delivered as frequently as possible.

- Don't buy bargain-priced supplies or materials you don't need at the moment.

- Analyze your needs and set stock points for each item in inventory. Avoid keeping stock "just in case." Such cases multiply, eating up cash and crowding space available.

- In large plants, Andersen Consulting maintains, it's best to create "subplants" each responsible for its own inventory. Doing so simplifies and speeds inventory handling.

> Avoid keeping stock "just in case." Doing so eats up cash.

- Buy items in volume but have your order delivered over the course of the year.

- Track carefully the inventory turnover ratio: cost of goods sold divided by average inventory. (You can also use net sales divided by average inventory.) Know the average inventory turn rate for your industry, and then use all your smarts to increase it. Cash sits locked in inventory waiting to get out.

Cycle times. This phrase usually refers to the time it takes to make a product and get it out the door. The shorter the better.

One reason cycle time is resistant to efforts to shorten it is that a number of departments, and sometimes companies, are involved. You need to optimize operations in each department—but not without maintaining an overview of the whole process. The chapter on reengineering (chapter nine) has a few ideas on improving cycle time.

Downtime rates. When machinery or facilities fail, everybody loses. A recent bomb scare at an IBM chip-making plant shut it for a day. Cost: $1 million. You probably needn't worry about a bomb scare, but all it takes is a key piece of machinery—or a network server—to fail and you have the potential for major losses.

The best inoculation against such losses is planned, preventive maintenance. That goes for computers as well as any production machinery. Ideally, this work is done at night or whenever use of the machine is lightest.

Best Tip

Planned, preventive maintenance can keep machines from going down at critical times.

Customer service. A really well-run customer service department is a joy to behold. Too many companies hire poorly and pay badly for customer-service positions. The long-term cost of that is excessive.

In well-managed customer service departments, workers are not only knowledgeable about the organization's products and policies, but they have the power to satisfy customers on the spot. This takes good hiring, even better training, and great information systems.

When well-trained and empowered, customer-service reps minimize the number of contacts a customer has with you over an order or problem. That shortens the time it takes to resolve a problem, keeps staffing needs stable, and shows customers you run a crisp, customer-centered operation.

Best Tip

Set challenging "speed up" goals. They'll force you to innovate in all areas of production.

Machine set-up times and changeovers. When it takes seven hours to set up a machine to make a product, it only makes sense to get in a long production run. Those long runs have a price. You build inventory you may not need, and it often forces you to make a standard product when the market may not want one.

Quick setup times and changeovers give you flexibility. You can do shorter runs, customize products for an important customer, and keep your machinery humming twenty-four hours a day.

Many manufacturers report setups or changeovers going from a matter of hours to minutes. The lower the figure, the more efficient you are—at a tremendous saving in cost.

Manufacturers also now use computer controls on machinery to maintain exact setup requirements. Using them allows a production run to begin immediately rather than starting with a long period of tweaking the dials to get a product just the way you want it.

Set Challenging Goals

Probably the only good way to speed up is to set challenging goals to do so. The stiffer the challenge, the better your results are likely to be. To get greatly improved results, you can't just polish an existing process; you have to think "out of the box."

Say, for example, you want to speed picking and packing an order from an average of three minutes down to one minute. Moving faster won't help. You'll have to redesign the process, invest in new equipment, or even redesign the warehouse. But the effort will be worth it.

In *Team Zebra*, a book about the turnaround of a division at Kodak, author Steve Frangos tells of a cycle-time reduction project for a particular film product. At the outset, cycle time was forty-two days. Actual value-adding time: *ten hours*. Product sat around in various stages of completion at a tremendous cost to Kodak.

Frangos and his people set a challenging goal that acted as a handy slogan: One day.

Team Zebra didn't get it down to one day—at least not by the end of the book—but they got it below twenty. That 50 percent reduction used all their ingenuity and resourcefulness. To succeed, the team reinvented the manufacturing process, and they did away with testing.

If process improvements were easy, somebody would have thought of them long ago. Speeding up is all about reinvention and innovation.

The Agile Manager's Checklist

✔ Speed up, in general, to keep costs at bay and increase productivity.

✔ Speed inventory turnover by holding fewer goods.

✔ Speed up customer service operations by training well and giving people the latitude to make decisions.

✔ Speed product development by having vendors join the design team.

Chapter Six

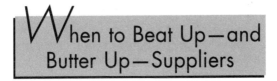

When to Beat Up—and Butter Up—Suppliers

"So Todd," said the Agile Manager. "You're willing to station one of your people here for three months, and then once again for a couple weeks once we start manufacturing?"

"Sure. I'm willing to give this a try. I'll need him back at the office maybe half a day a week. I'd still like to know what's going on."

"You can have him more than that, if you want. But if he's going to be part of the team, he'll be expected to be around for all the important events. And you know as well as I do that a lot of the important events are not scheduled—like a conversation around a picnic table that suddenly turns important."

"I understand. But I think just a half a day, like Thursday or Friday afternoons, is fine."

The Agile Manager paused and said, "You know what this means for you financially, right? Your own development costs will be much higher."

"I know." said Todd. "I've run the numbers ten different ways. And it always comes out looking good in the end, thanks to the volume we'll be running with you. And I also hope to learn a few tricks from your people."

"And don't think we won't be watching you—I've already assigned someone to buddy up with whoever you send over. I expect a good deal of cross-pollination."

"Let's just hope it all turns out like it does in books," said Todd. "You know—products developed faster, costs saved, better profits, better products, a long and prosperous relationship."

The Agile Manager heard a hint of skepticism sneak through Todd's confident tone.

If you listen to the experts, there are a couple of different ways to deal with vendors. You can play hardball with them, or you can work closely in a warm and fuzzy fashion.

Each side has its proponents, but I'm going to come down squarely on both sides. There's a time for hardball, and a time to play softball with squishy mitts.

Using the right approach at the right time can save large sums of money. It can also save you money by letting you slough off problems on others temporarily.

Hardball Tacticians

Some companies and some buyers play only hardball. They believe every salesperson or vendor firm is out to get them. Being tough as iron is the only way they know how to resist being taken advantage of.

Best Tip

There's a time to develop close relationships with vendors—and a time to play hardball.

Hardball negotiators, for instance, have no qualms about working closely with a vendor to come up with specs and a price for an item, then shopping those specs all over for the lowest price.

Hardball negotiators also love to keep holding out for one more contract point. Unless they get the last item changed in their favor, they've lost.

Hardball negotiators often bargain on price and price alone.

That's all that matters, in their view. Of course, that's usually the boss's view as well.

Is fighting over price always a good idea? Sometimes. But I once knew a lawyer who had a client that disputed every bill. To me, he just laughed about it. "I'll get him one way or another," he'd say. If he gave in on an item this time, he'd stick it in the next bill.

Hardball Players Damage Relationships—and Products

I once worked for a company that for a time dealt extensively with a local vendor. I would ask it to bid on projects. Then, at the behest of my boss, I'd show bids from competing high-volume out-of-state companies and say, "You get the job if you can match this quote."

For a while, this supplier did. But then it got tired of doing so—especially when we abused the relationship by taking forever to pay.

Nevertheless, the supplier con-

Best Tip

Don't become best friends with a salesperson at a vendor company. The friendship will cloud your judgment.

tinued to take on jobs to fill in slack time. The quality of the goods produced diminished. And why not? Its margin was so low that it put its least-experienced people on the job and avoided any quality control. It gave as good as it got, which wasn't much.

No one profited from the relationship, so it died. I learned a good lesson, but we lost a reliable partner who could do quick-turnaround jobs.

Avoid Cozy Relationships

I and another tough negotiator, Al Dunlap, are in the same camp on one issue: Too-close relationships with some suppliers. Dunlap writes in *Mean Business* that you know you have trouble when one of your own employees takes the side of a vendor in a minor dispute. In my experience, that happens all the time. ("Joe at Acme says they can't come down on price any further. I believe them. Besides, they promised us a quicker delivery to make up for the higher price.")

Good salespeople learn that they can make a nice living by becoming friends with buyers. They take them out to lunch and dinner, send cards on their children's birthdays, and go out of their way to be helpful on any issue. Such behavior isn't necessarily manipulative; it's a way salespeople grease the relationship's wheels.

Play hardball with airline, telephone, and car-rental companies.

The problem is, the more friendly you are with a vendor, the more you want to do business with it alone. And the less you take a critical view of their pricing or product quality. And, comfortable, you feel little need to go looking for alternative sources of supply.

Some companies will arbitrarily change suppliers every so often, just to ensure relationships between buyers and sellers don't get too close.

That may be extreme, but you should occasionally seek alternative prices for commodities or for any purchase over a certain amount of money. It's just too important to leave pricing to chance.

When to Play Hardball

Before we explore the soft side of buying and selling, let's look at when being a tough negotiator is the right thing to do:

When buying a commodity item or service. If you're paying 92 cents a gallon for fuel oil and everyone else is paying 86 cents, you're wasting money. It doesn't matter if you are buying it from your brother-in-law.

When dealing with telephone companies, airline carriers, and car-rental agencies. These organizations have, in my view, taught us to buy on price alone. And they take advantage of us when they can get away with it. Throw fast balls at their heads.

When buying cars or other company vehicles. Same as above. But don't get down in the mud with car and truck people. Have one of the new buying services find you the cheapest car available. Or use Price/Costco's prenegotiated pricing program. (I did, and with great success.)

When buying office supplies. Don't even see salespeople. Buy from warehouse stores, out of a catalog, or on the web.

When buying the services of some lawyers, consultants, and other providers of professional services. Notwithstanding my lawyer story above, some lawyers get way too far into your business. They plant the seed in your head that you'd better pass much of your work under their noses to stay out of trouble. This is rarely done crassly; just a little insinuation here, an aside there. Before long, you have junior counsel camped in your office. And you lose your will over time to keep their charges in check. Pay lawyers and consultants what they bill you, but keep them at arm's length. Beware, too, consultants who propose an absurd price for routine or speculative work.

When you buy something only once or infrequently. Go on, get the best price for a new copying machine. Have some fun doing it.

Best Tip

When a particular vendor is essential to your success, get cozy.

When buying something in huge numbers. It's only natural, I suppose, to use a large order as a club. But read the following sections before you do.

Reasons to Get Cozy with Vendors

There's one telling fact that crops up over and over in the business press. Large companies are cutting the number of vendors they deal with. And not just by 10 percent or so. Sometimes the cut is drastic.

A 3M plant, for instance, cut the number of its suppliers from 2,800 to 300. Ocean Spray cut the number of suppliers from 900 to 170. (And it purchases 90 percent of its goods from just

30 of these suppliers.) McKinsey & Company found that successful German manufacturers have 50-66 percent fewer suppliers than their less successful brethren. At some point they cut the number in a big way.

Common thinking used to be that having lots of suppliers is good. You can bounce them off each other for the best price, and if one goes under you always have another waiting to step in.

But enlightened companies have found that such thinking runs counter to their goals. When you buy on price, for one thing, the vendor might try to use cheaper materials or otherwise lower quality. And beating up suppliers does not result in loyal vendors. You need a rush order or special design work? Forget it.

So the thinking now is you can get great benefits by cutting down on the number of vendors, and dealing with those that remain much, much more closely.

How closely? This close: An industrial engineer at a large company was shocked to discover that one of his teammates, with whom he had worked for two years, was actually employed by a supplier.

More Reasons for Close Relationships

It's estimated that 60-65 percent of a product's production cost is made up of supplier parts and components. That's why it makes sense to work closely with suppliers. You can do a better job ensuring proper quality, and you can often work together to get prices down.

McDonnell-Douglas, for example, figures it cut about $300 million from the cost of a new plane by partnering with suppliers.

Another benefit: Think of the cost of negotiating and administering dozens or hundreds or thousands of contracts. Not to mention keeping inventory straight. Reduce the number of suppliers by half or more, and you've saved a ton of money.

That's not all. Vendors can help you succeed. They can, for instance, help you design and build part of a product. Daimler-Chrysler, which has saved lots of money by getting chummier with suppliers, lets vendors solve design problems on their own. With different groups inside the company and out working on design simultaneously, Chrysler gets new models into the market much faster. (And, not coincidentally, it has had the highest margins in the auto industry.)

Best Tip

Cut the number of suppliers you deal with. Get closer to the ones that are left.

Vendors can also teach you methods to control or enhance quality that you haven't thought of. Working together, you can figure out the most efficient way to supply or integrate parts.

Finally, with a close relationship, vendors will be a lot more loyal to you. That loyalty is largely based on increased business. If, say, you cut your suppliers for a key material or part from six to one or two, you will increase the volume you do with them. That may encourage them to retool or improve their processes—for your benefit. Prices often drop.

How to Get Close to Vendors

How do you establish closer ties—especially after years of adversarial relationships? Pick one or two vendors you've always worked well with and that deliver high-quality items or service.

Start at the top. Senior executives must get together and begin to establish trust. Hold discussions to uncover what the interests of each party are. Then try to figure out whether a closer relationship can satisfy these needs better.

Usually it can, for one good reason. You're joining together to satisfy a mutual concern: customers. If you both do well, you create more customers.

Be blunt. Tell the other firm that you will give it more business in exchange for what you believe will be a more fruitful relationship. Make clear what you want out of it—a better price, probably, and better quality. They'll get benefits, too—like new ideas and more business.

Furniture retailer Ikea, for instance, picks suppliers carefully. Then it helps them get better. It loans money or leases equipment at favorable rates. Its information system helps suppliers find the cheapest raw materials, and it matches them up with partners. Everyone wins—especially Ikea, which doesn't have to worry as much about what will fill its furniture showrooms.

Is establishing trust important? You bet. Often you will share information systems with suppliers, or they will need access to some of your trade secrets to do their work. Beyond trust, though, never forget to analyze what you are giving up to get.

And start slowly. There is a skill to working closely with outside organizations without losing sight of your own interests. Not to mention managing so things go smoothly. Remember—you won't be able to order vendor employees around, nor deny them needed resources. Your relationship will be complex, to say the least.

While friendships will develop, it's important to keep your eye on why you got into the close relationship—better quality, lower prices, and better work practices.

The Agile Manager's Checklist

✔ Don't play hardball with vendors all the time. You'll miss out on opportunities to save money and innovate.
✔ Don't let friendly salespeople blind you to issues of importance, like price and delivery.
✔ Get close, very close, with your most important vendors.
✔ Work to establish trust with key vendors.

Chapter Seven

Outsource To Save Money

.

"I don't see any reason we can't give it a try," said the Agile Manager. We'll delay one of our own products to make room for it. That'll save us around $75,000 this year."

Manuel and William, two ace product developers, looked grim and glum, respectively. Manuel, as usual, spoke first. "We're the ones who are supposed to come up with the good ideas. That's what we get paid for."

"And I'll continue to expect you to do that. But there are some pretty good solo product developers out there, and we've found one with a product concept worth playing around with. If any one of you had come to me with this project, I would've told you to move on it." He stopped for a moment. "Do either of you have a problem with it other than it wasn't invented here?"

"It doesn't exactly fit in with the line," said William. "It doesn't look like something we'd do."

"That's why we license the idea. We take the concept and mold it the way we want to. We'll make it look just like something we'd do."

"We don't get all the revenue, either, right?" asked Manuel.

"That's right," said the Agile Manager. "We pay a royalty. And *it's well worth it—he not only came up with a valuable idea, but he's got it in pretty good shape. We'll tweak it here and there, maybe redesign the housing and add a few minor features, then it's done. I'm really surprised someone working on the outside could come up with such a usable idea."*

Manuel and William continued to stare at the floor.

The Agile Manager said, in parting, "You two can take this thing and make it better. Once we come to terms with him, treat it as if it were your own."

Companies once strove to integrate vertically. They would attempt to do everything from producing raw materials to making things to distributing them. Henry Ford, for example, owned farms that produced the straw that eventually became Fordite, a key material in steering wheels.

Vertical integration is inefficient. A company simply cannot produce the best quality at the lowest prices in every area. Vertical integration inflates prices because it forces a company to purchase from captive companies, no matter what the cost.

Doubleday, for example, was the last large New York publisher to have its own printing presses. Doubleday executives had to face the daily indignity of paying printing costs far higher than if they could have shopped around.

Outsourcers Perform Better

The pendulum has swung in the opposite direction. Companies are outsourcing activities that once would have defined the firm's activities.

But it makes sense to outsource. Many companies you buy from have higher productivity in their area of specialty than you ever will. A common example: Why should any company run its own payroll operations when companies like ADP and others can do it faster, cheaper, and with fewer mistakes?

Outsourcing payroll is an easy decision for most. But you can go much farther. For example, more and more companies are using IBM or EDS to handle information processing needs. Some banks, for example, have hired IBM to handle their entire information technology infrastructure. IBM uses its own people—and its own equipment.

Navistar, the old International Harvester, will come in and take charge of your company's fleet shop, handling on a daily basis the repair and routine servicing of trucks and other vehicles.

The semiconductor company MIPS, now owned by Silicon Graphics, makes nothing. It pours all its resources into designing leading-edge RISC processing chips. Then it licenses these designs to other companies, like Toshiba and Philips, who make and sell them.

Best Tip

Outsource to capitalize on the advantages other companies bring to your market.

Gaining in popularity: leased employees. The staffing service that provides them takes a large burden off you—payroll, tax reporting, and benefits among other things. Plus, they can save you money through lower workers' compensation premiums, and they often provide employment liability insurance.

Where do trends in outsourcing lead? To the virtual company, which we'll discuss in chapter ten.

Save Costs by Outsourcing

One of the main advantages of outsourcing is cost savings. Say you lease your staff from an outside company. Suddenly you need fewer accountants and bookkeepers, your CPA spends less time preparing tax returns, you shut down your human resources department, and you lay off redundant supervisors.

In the Continental example above, recall, the bank let IBM handle all the equipment. No need for repair technicians or an army of auditors keeping track of depreciation.

Worried about those losing their jobs? It's been shown conclusively that your knowledge workers—researchers, managers, in-house service providers—will have no trouble finding work elsewhere. When a large company like AT&T sheds experienced telecom engineers, Silicon Valley companies stand ready to snap them up. And they do.

First to Go: Support Services

Support services in organizations are usually monopolies. These include in-house advertising departments, maintenance, information technology, and legal services. Interestingly, while manufacturing productivity rises yearly, white-collar productivity remains flat or decreases.

Why? Monopolies usually have no incentive to improve productivity. Nor must they view the users of their services as customers that must be satisfied. It's likely the maintenance-services manager thinks more in terms of increasing yearly budgets than in increasing a company's profit by reducing costs.

Outside firms in support services have an entirely different view. They work to improve productivity and serve the customer better, because they know that a company can drop their services any time. If they want work, they must perform.

ServiceMaster, for example, provides housecleaning services for many hospitals. It works actively to reduce the time it takes to do a job, and it does R&D to produce better tools. Service-Master employees can make a hospital bed faster than anyone. And they work with special brooms and dusters designed specifically for the job and the setting they work in. Few in-house cleaning services have the budget or inclination to improve work practices in that manner. Their solution to most problems is to throw more people at the job.

Best Tip

Outsource such things as payroll, maintenance, and information technology first.

Outsourcers like ServiceMaster also attract better workers. That's because those who start at the bottom in such organizations know they can advance into management. Can that be said of workers employed by your in-house support services?

Don't Outsource Everything

Whatever you do, don't outsource the things that give you a competitive advantage. Some people feel IBM made a major mistake, for instance, by outsourcing the PC's operating system to Microsoft (not to mention the microprocessor to Intel). Microsoft supplied DOS, which gave it a broad base of revenue with which to bring out other products. The rest is history.

Best Tip

Go slowly with outsourcing. It can increase the complexity of your business immensely.

Many publishers now outsource editorial work. They buy "packaged" books from vendors who commission the writing of the book, edit and design it, make up pages, and in some cases arrange for printing. If editorial judgment and production capabilities are not the unique competitive advantage of a publishing company, what are? (To be fair, some publishers view their expertise as distribution—doing nothing more than filling the pipeline they've created.)

Before you outsource, think long and hard about the ramifications one, five, and ten years out. If you let a supplier produce a key component of a product, will it get a stranglehold over you or turn into a competitor?

And remember, your advantage may not be in the ultimate product or service. It may be in your in-house efficiencies, logistics, distribution, design, or your very skill in finding the best partners to do the work.

Last, outsourcing many different elements of your business system may increase the complexity of managing it all. The effort it takes to coordinate the activities of many subcontractors and their interactions with you may not be worth the results, even if they are good.

How to Outsource

Good all-purpose advice: Move slowly into outsourcing. Dealing with a number of separate organizations gets complicated.

Begin with high-level contacts between companies, and make sure everyone knows what each party wants out of the arrangement. In addition:

- Build cost containment into the deal. You don't want to be held hostage by an outside organization. Beyond price, be sure the outsourcer can provide the quality you need.
- Investigate the outsourcer carefully (especially overseas manufacturing facilities). You want to make sure it is willing to invest in R&D and process improvement for your benefit. Some companies hire third parties to check on the outsourcer's costs and work practices.
- Make sure an outsourcer can meet your production schedule.
- Have contingency plans if your relationship with an outsourcer sours. Always leave yourself an out.
- If the outsourcer will be in on trade secrets, consider some sort of non-compete agreement.
- Put the right people on the job of working with key outsourcers. Put abrasive, command-and-control-type managers at the bottom of your list.
- Anticipate and plan to neutralize in-house resistance to the deal. Some managers may be upset that you're giving away work they feel they can do.

The Agile Manager's Checklist

✔ Off-load a good bit of your work—and expense— through the outsourcing of tasks and operations.
✔ Outsource support services first.
✔ Begin slowly with outsourcing. Start at the top, and build cost-containment into the deal.

Chapter Eight

Keep Headcount Low

The Agile Manager sat staring at his computer screen late in the afternoon. The spreadsheet contained some of the numbers he tracked regularly.

One of those numbers, sales per employee, always looked good to him. At an organizational level, they were among the best in the industry at $460,000 per. That was due to the CEO's mantra— "People are expensive. Pay those you have well, and work them hard. Use outsiders when you can."

The Agile Manager couldn't argue with that philosophy. He hated a few of the organizations he'd worked in because they had too many people. When people have time on their hands, they snipe and play political games. And the nonproducers demoralize those who want to be productive.

Lean headcount, he said to himself, sure made things easier now. The trouble in Asia was of monumental proportions. The company was shuttering a two-year-old factory due to not one but five or six serious problems. The government was corrupt, the workforce couldn't or wouldn't learn their jobs, the native managers had been making side deals to produce items for friends, and on and on. How, he wondered, could our people have watched while all this went on?

That's grist for a Harvard case study, and not my concern. But if this company hadn't been lean to begin with, we might have been looking at 10 or 15 percent across-the-board cuts. And the whole company might now be at risk.

All the hoops you have to jump through here to hire—especially quantifying each hire as an investment and showing the payoff—makes it awfully hard to add new people. A good thing, too.

People are expensive. You pay them a salary. You offer benefits. You pay taxes on them. They take up space. They use equipment. If you fire them and they get mad, they may try to sue you.

In his 1993 book *No-Excuses Management*, T. J. Rodgers, head of Cypress Semiconductor, estimated how much it cost to employ a person. The average salary and benefits at Cypress at the time totaled $50,000. With the buildup of bodies, he reasoned, you eventually needed someone to manage them at $75,000. In addition, Each person used $25,000 worth of office space, computer, telephone, office furniture, and so on, each year. It cost $4,000 a year to maintain those things.

Thus, adding an employee cost Cypress around $100,000 a year in the early 1990s. It isn't any cheaper now.

Yet people are more than a matter of dollars and cents. Without them you wouldn't have a company. Don't fall into the trap some academic business writers do and look at human resources as one "factor" of many in a company; people *are* the business.

Watch Key Measures

Just like T. J. Rodgers, you need to know the cost of adding a person to the payroll. That figure alone may shock you enough to stop you from hiring.

Here's where watching figures like revenues or profits per employee is helpful. Your job as a manager is to help bring either figure up. When you add an employee, you must be reasonably certain that the cost will be more than offset by additional revenues or lower costs. If neither situation results, that extra person will be sharing in funds already employed—to pay you, pay for research, and pay others. There will be fewer resources for all, and the company will suffer.

Another measure worth watching is the employee compensation ratio, which is your payroll divided by net sales. For example, say you have 125 people who cost an average of $58,000 a year in salary, benefits, and taxes. That's a total payroll cost of $7.25 million. You have $22 million in sales, so employee expenses are 33 percent of sales.

Best Tip

Add up how much each employee costs in salary, benefits, equipment, space used, etc. It'll open your eyes.

This ratio varies widely from industry to industry, so compare it with others in your industry. If it's high compared with others, lower it. Your competition is selling more with fewer people (or else paying them a lot less).

Put Controls on Hiring

In a nutshell, make it damn hard to hire additional people. Hiring should be the last resort.

Sometimes adding people is a difficult decision. For example, it's hard to decide to add a person speculatively—say, to grow part of the business or in anticipation of growth that may or may not occur.

Other times the decision is easy. It's clear that you could sell more if you had more people on the production line.

I've worked in places where managers said, "We need another person," and hired. Often this turned out badly, because they thought only vaguely about how the workflow would change with a new person involved. Sometimes they didn't reason through what the new person would do all day. And they never stopped to figure out whether the hire would result in offsetting revenues or costs saved.

Quantify your decision to hire, and be able to justify it: "If we add this person, at a total yearly cost of around $80,000, we will add at least $110,000 in revenues. Here's how I arrived at that figure . . ."

The rule of thumb, again: watch revenue or profits per employee. Make sure adding staff causes neither figure to decline.

Alternatives to Hiring People

Here are ways you can get more work done without hiring:

Outsource. Go back and read the last chapter. Also, never hire someone full-time for a job that needs to be done only occasionally. There are hundreds of speech writers, for example, who work as independent contractors. And your city has an army of graphic designers who would love to help you create a logo, design and produce a brochure, or do your newsletter each month. Get this kind of work done outside the organization—outsourcers will do it better, faster, and cheaper.

Hire temps. But only for real crunch periods and for jobs easy to learn. Temps tend to be viewed by most as second-class employees and aren't as productive as your regular employees.

Some managers feel temps aren't worth the trouble and never use them. Their thinking: "We either have a job for which we should hire someone full-time, or we don't."

Eliminate work. Companies often have people—and sometimes whole departments—that do work that doesn't need to be done. People produce reports that don't get read, attend meetings that waste time, do hand calculations as a backup to work done on computers, and serve on committees that don't have a chance of getting their recommendations approved. Look askance at any work that doesn't directly support your company's mission. Ask, "Does this matter to the customer?"

Best Tip
The best way to keep expenses and headcount down: Eliminate work.

Buy a machine. Machines don't demand generous benefits, take lunch breaks, or go on vacation. If you can automate, do so. But not before you're sure you are doing work the most efficient way.

Upgrade equipment, especially computers. If you're still working on old 486-class computers, it's time to upgrade. If you see people hanging around a network printer, get a fast production printer. If they cluster around

---
Best Tip

When it comes to necessary technology, spare no expense.

---

fax machines, supply them with modems and teach them to fax direct from the desktop.

Remember, anything you can do to speed operations cuts costs. And work tirelessly to remove impediments to employees' ability to add value.

Banish offices (for some). Give your salespeople or consultants laptop computers, car phones, and e-mail accounts. Tell them you don't, in general, want to see them. (You'll still be watching the tracks they make.) The cost of "carrying" road employees will be slightly lower than those in the office—and a lot lower if the strategy ever eliminates the need for larger quarters. And your road warriors should be more productive.

Also, consider letting people work at home. Though doing so may take a leap of faith on your part, most studies show that people working at home are more productive than they are at the office. There's less to distract them.

More productive means people do more work. If they do more work, you can hold steady the number of people employed. Bonus: You'll spend less on office furniture and, sometimes, equipment. Double bonus: Your people will be happier.

Get Rid of Nonproducers

I've never seen a company that didn't occasionally harbor nonproducers. At better companies, they root out parasites quickly. At poor companies, nonproducers not only stay warm and happy in their cozy nests, but they sometimes get put in charge of other parasites.

All this is tremendously demoralizing for those who want to do a good job and get ahead, as most employees do. And the team's work suffers. Nonproducers not only poison the whole bunch with a bad attitude, but they impede the flow of work.

If you don't know who the nonproducers in your area are, you're not paying attention. Out them by giving stiff—but fair—deadlines for real work. They'll try to cover their lacks by squawking loudly about the workload. And they'll miss deadlines. Then you've got them.

The Agile Manager's Checklist

✔ Hire only when you're pushed to the wall. Analyze beforehand how you'll pay for the person.
✔ Cut unnecessary employees. They'll find work.
✔ Value all the more highly employees you keep.
✔ Use ratios like sales per employee to see how your staffing levels compare with others in the industry.

Organizationwide Cost-Cutting

*"To make strength productive is the
unique purpose of organization."*

PETER F. DRUCKER
IN *THE EFFECTIVE EXECUTIVE*

Chapter Nine

Reengineer—Maybe

The Agile Manager, feet propped up on his desk and enjoying the late afternoon sun in his office, put down the magazine. The article, covering a variation on reengineering that tried to make it seem new and effortless, made him think back wistfully to his first great boss, Dick Jonas.

Jonas, long before anyone ever heard the word reengineering, was great at it. "Look at this," he said once, shoving a napkin toward the Agile Manager. "That shows how we're moving stuff in and out the door." The drawing on the napkin, complicated and disorganized, showed lines stretched in convoluted patterns to and from blocks labeled warehousing, inventory reconciliation, accounting, packing, receiving, and others. It nevertheless reflected reality. "This one," he said, flipping the napkin over, "shows how it could be done." The new drawing was neater, simpler, cleaner—and unassailable. It combined steps, simplified them, and made perfect logical sense.

"Want to help me see if a drawing bears any relation to reality?" asked Jonas with a twinkle in his eye.

That event was memorable. Jonas made some real changes, and he showed how a deft human-relations touch greased the wheels of progress. For instance, he got computers out on the load-

ing dock, which not only updated inventory figures instantly but cleared invoices for payment. That could have riled managers who stood to lose (and ultimately did) the number of clerks working for them, were it not for the way Jonas presented it. Like a magician, he showed how everything he proposed would not only benefit the company, but each manager as well.

Things didn't work out just like Jonas's drawing, but the company cut order-fulfillment time by six days and cut costs in every department associated with it. As the company grew and prospered, everyone, just as Jonas predicted, prospered with it.

Nothing caught the business world with so much force a few years ago than did the concept of reengineering. It's easy to see why—it was easy to understand, and it promised so much for so little. Reengineering said, "I'll take your inefficient business processes and rework them almost effortlessly, and in the end you'll save loads of time and money."

We should have been suspicious. If something is easy to do, people do it, reap the benefits, and get on to the next improvement.

Yet reengineering does work. People do it all the time. And they did it long before Hammer and Champy came along, in *Reengineering the Corporation*, with their new word for an old business practice.

What Reengineering Is

A reengineering project reinvents and improves dramatically a process. Processes are companywide, cross-functional efforts like filling an order from start to finish, developing products, converting a prospect into a customer, and providing after-sale service, to name a few. The end of a process is always a result that somehow meets customer needs.

Cyberguru James Martin, coming from a slightly different slant, calls processes "value streams." He defines these as end-to-end activities that together deliver a satisfying result to customers. Besides the processes mentioned above, he includes in his list of value streams things like financial management, procurement services, and the application of information technology.

Why reengineer? Over time, processes become inefficient, often consisting of jury-rigged operations that people added to deal with new situations. Most processes, maintain the experts, could use redesigning and retooling. And when you do, dramatic improvements result.

The Problem with Reengineering

With all the hype, people figured reengineering was a can't-miss proposition. Managers rushed into reengineering projects, egged-on by consultants, and soon found that the perfect-world, blank-slate approach rarely worked.

Why? Among the reasons:

- People often had good reason to do things the way they always did;
- Many resisted reengineering, figuring they'd only be putting themselves out of work;

The blank-slate approach advocated by reengineering enthusiasts rarely works in the real world.

- Managers who implemented reengineering treated it as just another fad that—like other fads—looked good on the surface but did little to change underlying work practices or structure;
- Parts of the process took place in different locations and were hard to bring together;
- Optimizing one process sometimes totally fouled up another;
- Managing the people who were affected by what was sometimes severe disruption to the workplace was darned hard.

The sad fact is that reengineering is considered by many a failure. Most studies come up with the same appalling statistic: Managers are disappointed with the results of about 70 percent of all reengineering efforts. That's usually because they never produced the returns promised, but also because some reengineering projects are grossly disruptive to the organization.

What's more, a few years after the reengineering craze swept the business world, Gary Hamel and C. K. Prahalad came along in *Competing for the Future* to remind managers that reengineering, even if successful, was the equivalent of cleaning out the garage. Sure, you could clean up a process, make it more orderly, and cut some costs, but is that what business is for?

Of course not. The purpose of business is to create new products that create new customers. Time spent reengineering was time spent focused inwardly instead of identifying and satisfying customer needs.

Reengineering Happens

Reengineering has been done for years by managers who look at the work they do and wonder, "Can we do this job better? Should we do it at all?" Also, technology often revolutionizes a process. No one has to stop to think about whether changing how they do things is a good idea or not; it's clear that change is worth the expense.

Here's an example. In publishing, I've watched as the industry reengineered the whole prepress process—the string of events that stretch from the writing of a book to getting it to the printer.

Here's how the process used to work. Writers produced a paper manuscript using a typewriter. The publisher would take the

Best Tip

The purpose of business isn't to become efficient above all else. It's to create customers.

manuscript, edit it, then pass it along to a typesetter. The typesetter keystroked the whole thing all over again. The publisher then got galleys—long pages of type—back from the typesetter. It proofread the galleys against the edited manuscript, then sent them back to the typesetter for corrections.

Once the corrected text came back, a page-makeup artist cut the type into pages, pasted it down on cardboard, and sent it back. If the publisher was lucky, there were just enough words to fill the number of pages allotted. If not, the writer wrote more or the editor cut words. Either way, the typesetter got involved again and the page makeup person had to pull up sections of type and reconfigure them. And every time the typesetter got involved again, you proofread.

> **Best Tip**
>
> Technology often revolutionizes a process—long before anyone gets around to "reengineering" it.

After a few rounds of this activity, the publisher would finally declare victory and send the cardboard pages to the printer. The printer's first step would be to take a picture of each page.

This sounds, and was, horribly inefficient. But only in retrospect. None of us knew any different. So editors got good at predicting the number of pages, and page makeup artists learned to fudge in their jobs to better accommodate the inevitable changes.

Look how things have changed: Writers write on computers, and they send a disk to the publisher (or they e-mail files). The publisher takes the file and edits and proofreads on-screen. A production person takes the file, imports it into a page-makeup program, and formats the book. You know instantly whether you're too long or too short, and it's far, far easier to adjust the text to the length of the book.

Typesetters and old-fashioned page-makeup artists are history. And printers take the work on disk, sometimes going straight to printing plate from it. That eliminates at least one step on their end, and sometimes two or three.

This is, clearly, a reengineered process. And it would have occurred with or without Hammer and Champy.

The Elements of a Reengineered Process

Let's identify the characteristics of a process improvement job, based on my story above:

- *You combine jobs.* Our production person, remember, now does the job of both the typesetter and page makeup artist.
- *You eliminate steps.* No rekeying of the manuscript, for one thing. No laborious paste up of the type.
- *You optimize the process across boundaries.* We've even saved the printer a step or two, for goodness' sake.
- *All the work is done in a central location.* All the important work (save the initial writing) is done where it should be—in the publishers' office.
- *Steps are done in a more logical order.* With the old process, recall, there was a lot of back and forth between publisher, typesetter, author, and makeup artist. A book is now produced in a much more orderly fashion.
- *The operation is as small and complete as possible.* In my example, there are no wasted steps.
- *You save a lot of money.* That was inevitable, given the number of steps we removed.

A Modest Formula for Reengineering

While reengineering often happens on its own (you either change or go out of business), it's often worthwhile to jumpstart the process by looking around for operations to improve. But before you start, make sure you have senior managers behind the effort.

One of the problems with reengineering is that there's no real formula for doing it. Every operation, every company, and every industry are different. (Maybe Andersen Consulting does have a formula, but it hasn't yet told me what it is.)

Nonetheless, here's a short list of guidelines for getting results. Don't forget that these guidelines, like the concept of reengineering itself, make it look easy. It's not.

1. Choose a process to reengineer. Keep in mind that it's not worth killing yourself to reengineer some operations—perhaps how you deal with waste. Take on those processes that affect customers directly, like marketing, or product development.

2. Create a reengineering team. It should be composed mostly of people that work in that process (and in a variety of functions). You want buy-in from the people who will be involved, and they know better than anyone how things are currently done. Include someone with clout to clear away organizational roadblocks. Finally, if you can, put a person who has done the job elsewhere (or a consultant) on the team. She has valuable experience.

3. Map the process. Map it from start to finish in excruciating detail. Include branches or subprocesses. Your goal is to become intimate with the process and the people and departments that take part in it.

Best Tip

There is no recipe for reengineering. Every industry, company, and process is different.

4. Improve the process. You'll have to come up with measures that track the efficiency of the process as is and goals for what will be. Likely candidates include productivity measures, cycle times, and cost.

How to improve it? Use your wits and imagination. Aim to accomplish the things mentioned above—combine or eliminate steps, reorganize the work into a more orderly fashion, and eliminate checking, testing, or control steps.

If you can, contain the operation in a smaller area. This may be difficult. When Kodak tried to redesign the "flow" (process of finishing film from start to finish) in its Black & White film division, it discovered that the flow spanned nine buildings—and two states and four countries!

One valuable improvement method gets mentioned by the experts frequently: Design a process as though one person were doing it. The reason for going through this exercise is not because one person can do it all, but because the "one person test" helps you see where there is waste and inefficiency.

If, for example, a customer service person has to take an order over the phone, key it into the computer, then print it out and walk it a hundred yards into the next building, a reasonable person might wonder, "What do I have do all that for? Can't I just key in the order and send it electronically to shipping?" Well? Can she?

5. Make sure your work pays off. Have you reached your financial or productivity goals? Why not?

Use Technology

The experts agree on one point: Reinvent your process first, then use technology to speed it up or otherwise enhance the results you're seeking. If you start with technology, you may end up automating inefficient practices.

But it's in technology that you get the "dramatic improvements" we're all searching for. In improving its customer-service process, insurer USAA got rid of paper altogether. Its mailroom people scan the documents it receives into the company's network and shred the paper. USAA saves money in eliminating filing and storage space, but the revised process delivers an even more important benefit. Customer-service reps can view the files on any customer from any work station. They never have to say, "Let me go get the file," or, "Sorry, I can't get at the file right now." The odds are that the rep can solve a problem or answer a question on the spot.

The Agile Manager's Checklist

✔ Be suspicious of any new management technique that promises huge returns for modest efforts.
✔ To begin revamping a process, pretend only one person will be doing the job from top to bottom.
✔ Reengineer before you automate.

Chapter Ten

Restructure Work Continuously

"I'm taking Anita off the 1800 Diagnosticator," said the Agile Manager.

Wanda's mouth opened but nothing came out. Finally she said, "Why? It's our most profitable product, and she's our best designer."

"Right on both counts," he said grinning. "The 1800 is a cash cow. But the 2800 and 3200 both can now do much of what it does, and a lot more. I don't believe that the 1800 has much life left."

Wanda stilled looked incredulous. "Then we should have Anita give it a major makeover."

"Why?" asked the Agile Manager. "The 1800 is a third-generation machine and we're on to the fourth generation. Some of its longtime fans will continue to buy it as long as it's around, but I'm sure the 2800 and 3200 will overtake it in the next couple years. Especially if we add a few features. It's time to put the 1800 out to pasture—before someone else does it for us."

He looked up at the ceiling briefly. "Besides, Anita is too good to keep on a project like that. Why use our best talent to keep a product propped up? She needs to be on the 3200—or maybe even that way-out sonar analyzer Phil had to shelve a while ago.

She's real creative in the way she can think of new uses for prod-ucts that none of us can—especially customers."

Wanda got up and headed toward the door. "I've got to let this sink in a bit," she mumbled.

Robert Sibson, an expert in both productivity improvement and compensation, relates a startling statistic in one of his books. It seems that back around the end of World War II, 80 percent of all the employees in a company were producers. They did something that contributed directly to the products or services the organization sold.

Sibson now puts that figure at about 50 percent. The rest are managers, support staff, and other hangers-on.

Despite what many see as a huge and heartless bloodletting, the restructurings of the past decades often benefited companies that had grown fat on a diet of marginally productive workers.

Restructurings Done Poorly

Unfortunately, many companies that slimmed down botched the job. They needed to cut costs, so they targeted the most expensive item in the company—people.

Companies often restructured without giving two thoughts to reducing the amount and kind of work those people were doing. As a result, productivity declined, and demoralized workers tried to do the work of two. Costs went up, too, because companies hired outsiders to do the work once done inside.

Best Tip

When you downsize, reduce or eliminate work. If you don't, you'll never see any financial benefits.

Restructuring, strictly speaking, is not about letting people go. It's about analyzing the work you're doing and deciding whether it supports directly the products or services you're selling.

Restructuring thus has to do with setting long-term goals, financial and otherwise, and configuring the organization to reach them. You stop, look around, and ask, are we doing the right things? Do we have the right people to do them? Do we have the right number of people to do them? How might we reorganize our operations to reach goals more efficiently?

Best Tip

You can restructure without downsizing. Companies adding staff restructure often.

Eliminate Work, Not Jobs

Companies often restructure without cutting jobs. Microsoft is a good example. Bill Gates has said that he sponsors a major restructuring about every two years. He believes it's necessary to take advantage of current opportunities. A good example? Microsoft's agile shift to an Internet focus. (Gates also uses restructurings to expose people to new areas—like moving product designers closer to customers by putting them in marketing.)

Despite the frequent restructurings, Microsoft hasn't been cutting jobs. It has been adding them at breakneck speed. But people are shifted, and jobs added, where opportunities lie. Gates heeds well Peter Drucker's dictum to "starve the problems and feed the opportunities."

Companies build up costs unnecessarily by feeding problems. They throw resources—including effective people—at work that probably shouldn't be done. Companies also strive mightily to keep mature cash-producing products strong, when a better strategy is to work hard to create new cash cows.

What Work to Cut

Many of the chapters have touched on eliminating work, like avoiding redundancies by optimizing operations, and eliminating reports that no one reads and meetings that serve no purpose.

Those kinds of things are the low-hanging fruit. They are easy to pick. Harder, much harder, is deciding to cut work when the people doing it seem to be busy and productive. It's in cutting whole operations, however, that you get the major benefits—the most costs reduced and the most resources freed to use elsewhere.

Best Tip

Every so often, ask about an operation: "Should we still be doing this? What if we stopped doing it?"

One way to focus on productive work and eliminate distractions is to create a set schedule to evaluate all you do. Every few years—or less, if you're in a high-tech industry—you ask, "Do we need to do this work? Why? What would happen if we stopped doing it?"

If the answers to these questions are, respectively, "Absolutely!" "It's the lifeblood of the company!" and "The company would fall apart!" fine. Continue doing the work. But if it takes you more than a few minutes to consider why you should continue to do a certain operation or maintain a questionable product line, that may be a signal that you've lost your focus.

Many companies practice a program of planned obsolescence. 3M strives to get 30 percent of its revenues from products introduced in the past four years. You can't achieve a goal like that without concentrating on opportunities at the expense of mature products.

All this applies to operations as well as products. What contribution is the operation supposed to make to the company? Is that contribution still valid? Is the operation succeeding? If not, question its value.

It also applies to divisions or whole companies under a corporate umbrella. When Al Dunlap took over as CEO of Scott Paper, one of the first things he did was to sell paper manufacturer S. D. Warren, a multibillion dollar enterprise. Dunlap decided Scott needed to focus on consumer products, not paper.

Barriers to Eliminating Work

Making such decisions is easier said than done. One major reason is that certain people—sometimes key senior managers, even the CEO—are tied to successes they had a hand in. They aren't keen to divert resources used to support that success.

Another reason is concern for the workforce. Even if an operation or product group isn't worth supporting, what about the people that work for it? Microsoft and other leading companies find other places to put good people. But if a company's leadership is focused on the past and present, there may be nowhere for them to go. As long as things remain profitable, they stay. But when indicators head south, the blood bath begins.

Semco, a Brazilian manufacturer known for its innovative attitude in all corners of its businesses, puts the burden on senior managers to make operations succeed. If a division is in decline, Semco will let everyone involved go—even good managers who were in the wrong place at the wrong time. But everyone knows how things work at Semco, so people strive to succeed.

Where to Save Major Costs

Here's a list of ideas for creating major savings:

Eliminate operations. Some people believe cutting costs permanently is possible only by eliminating whole operations. Peter Drucker maintains that as much as a third of clerical operations, and a third of control operations, are unneeded. If true, that leaves you a lot of room to cut. (In such cases you may need to let people go permanently.)

Best Tip

Companies with lots of managers are probably headed downhill.

Cut management levels. If your company is still thick with nonproducing managers, somebody, soon, will eat your lunch. You're slower than you need to be, and probably more rigid. The more managers, the more controls get put into place.

These guidelines indicate how many management levels make sense:

- Small companies (one to a hundred employees): two or three levels;
- Medium-sized companies (one hundred to a thousand): three to five levels;
- Large companies (over a thousand): five to seven levels.

If in doubt, err on the lower end of the range.

Ax quality control and checking functions. Checking up on products or people is time-consuming and hence costly. The most successful companies often do neither. They build quality into the manufacturing process through tight operations and computer controls, and they hire trustworthy people.

Abolish clerical help. Semco did. Despite the grumbling, doing so paid rich dividends. Managers wrote fewer memos and letters, meaning those they wrote tended to be important. Fewer documents meant less copying, less filing, and fewer meetings on inconsequential matters.

Cross-train people within departments. Turn department personnel or those tied to a particular operation into teams. Have teammates learn everyone else's job. Done right, structuring by team probably means you will need fewer people to do the same amount of work—and no need to bring in temps or subs when a team member is sick or on vacation.

Bosses: Give your division heads autonomy and financial goals. Hold them accountable for reaching goals.

Decentralize. This can be synonymous with cutting management levels, but not always. Some CEOs simply give the heads of divisions or companies financial and other goals and let them meet these goals however they want. If they don't meet goals, the CEO brings in new management.

The paradigm of hands-off management is Warren Buffett's

Berkshire Hathaway. Buffett has no interest in running, or meddling in, the companies Berkshire owns.

Many companies have gone from huge headquarters staff and thousands of square feet in office space to comparatively small numbers in both areas. Swiss-Swedish conglomerate ABB, for example, has a tiny headquarters staff; each company owned by ABB is relatively autonomous.

Organize by process or product. Some companies have banished functional fiefdoms and organized around cross-functional processes, like product development and manufacturing. Or they make a product the focus of a cross-functional team. Doing so puts the emphasis on the activities that deliver results to outside customers, which promotes "lean thinking." Support staff can't build up as fast.

Best Tip

Organize around a process or a product rather than by function.

The Virtual Organization

Some very nimble companies are much less than they seem to be. They are virtual.

A virtual company is one that appears to be bigger than it is. It's usually run by a small group of people who contract out whole segments of its operation. It leaves for itself only the tasks that make it competitive.

Consider The Benetton Group, the Italian manufacturer of sweaters and other clothing. Benetton has seven thousand stores worldwide. It must need an army of managers to supervise the stores, dozens of factories to churn out the sweaters, and a large headquarters staff managing the operation, right?

Wrong. Benetton owns only a few of the stores. The rest of them hold licenses to merchandise Benetton clothing and other items. And while more than 450 factories make Benetton clothing, the company owns only a few. (One of them, however, is a real humdinger. Benetton's highly automated complex in Treviso,

Italy, is capable of churning out 100 million garments a year.)

What does Benetton do? Three things, and all extraordinarily well. First, it designs sweaters people want to buy. Second, it uses custom information technology to link stores in its empire. The system feeds headquarters with real-time sales information from each store. Benetton knows, up to the instant, what designs are selling, which colors are most popular and in which sizes, and the level of a store's stock.

Best Tip

If you go virtual, plan to wire your firm to the maximum internally, as well as to vendors and the marketplace.

It uses this information to stay on top of fashion trends, and also to coordinate manufacturing facilities. Orders are transmitted, for example, three times daily to the manufacturers who make particular products.

Third, it leverages its use of technology. Its automated distribution system, for example, is capable of shipping 30,000 packages daily—and with a staff of only nineteen people! It estimates a conventional system would need over 400 people to ship the same number of orders.

Benetton also appears larger through creative licensing of the Benetton name. It licenses the name for such thing as watches, perfume, and even condoms.

The benefits of such virtuality include:

- You move far faster than large, lumbering organizations laden with bureaucracy.
- Your suppliers do what they do best, leaving you to worry about the activities that give you an edge.
- You run a sizable firm with a modest number of employees.
- You can start a company and keep it going using much less capital.
- You share the risk (and the rewards) with supplier firms.

Some companies have always been virtual. Construction companies, for example, succeed by maintaining a small, core staff who do two things really well: estimating costs and knowing how to run a job so it gets done on time and within budget. They add people when they get a job, and let them go when the job ends.

It's probably best for a company to start virtual, rather than to become virtual. And the jury is still out on whether virtual companies have a better chance of long-term success than their more traditional competitors.

The Agile Manager's Checklist

✔ Restructure to become more efficient and to respond to the market, not merely to cut headcount.

✔ Set revenue goals that include a percentage from new products. That encourages innovation.

✔ Learn to get along without secretaries or file clerks.

✔ To become virtual, save for yourself the tasks that make you competitive. Outsource or license the rest.

Chapter Eleven

Create Budgets— For Everything

"Keep a file," said Chuck, the accountant, "with a folder for each account you control. In each folder, keep notes that help you come up with better numbers each time you prepare a budget."

The Agile Manager, his hands forming a pyramid, nodded slowly.

"For instance," said Chuck, "you have an account here called Blueprints. I assume you have some of them done by our people, and some done out of house, right?"

"Actually, I think we have our people do most of them."

"Well, you need to introduce some competition, then. No one forces you to use our people, and most departments needing blue-prints use different sources. Competition is good for our support staff, anyway—keeps 'em on their toes. Anyway, if you had a folder for your blueprints account, you'd stuff it with figures—cop-ies of invoices, or maybe just a spreadsheet that noted the date of the expenditure, who produced the prints, how much it cost, and a running total. I like to keep copies of invoices when possible—I look for such things as turnaround time, hourly rate, fees tacked on for rush jobs, and so forth. Then I can evaluate vendors and com-pare them with in-house services."

He paused, to see if the Agile Manager wanted to say any-

thing. Apparently not, so he continued. "That kind of knowledge helps you make more cost-effective decisions about whom to use and when. And it helps you make better estimates for the coming year. You can even come up with little ratios to ease the job. For instance, say historically you spend X amount per project on blueprints. This year, you know you have Y products to enhance or develop, so you multiply Y by X to get a reasonable estimate. Am I making sense?"

"Of course—and it's very helpful. You also mentioned something about building productivity goals into the budget . . ."

It's such an obvious concept: Set financial goals like a 6 percent return on sales or a 3 percent improvement in productivity. Estimate the costs that will get you there. Set a budget. Adhere to it. Meet your goals.

Most companies maintain some kind of budgeting process. A sizable minority don't.

Lack of budgeting is a problem mostly in smaller businesses.

Best Tip

No matter how small your company, create a budget and stick to it.

Large companies, especially those publicly held, know how important it is to meet their numbers each quarter. The only way to do that is through careful sales forecasting and budgeting.

Budgeting Starts at the Top

The will to budget must start at the top of the organization. If senior managers don't create budgets, or if they pay them lip service only and deviate from them at will, those below them do the same.

Budgets can't be created out of thin air. They are the direct result of good financial and strategic management. Somebody, some time, has to say, "This is what we are going to do. This is how we are going to do it. Here's how we will spend money to reach our objectives."

The budget thus reflects close analysis of the marketplace and how well the company can perform in it. It requires a sound understanding of the company's capabilities and what costs will help it reach its sales potential.

The budget then becomes a yardstick. Each number not met—revenue or cost—is a red flag that causes good managers to think, "Are our assumptions wrong? Where? How can we set them straight?" And, if assumptions are sound, "We've got to rein in costs there or boost sales here. Let's get cracking."

Senior managers also need to be involved in budgeting beyond setting goals and broad budgeting guidelines. They have to judge among the competing requests for more money. If department A wants to hire three people, and department B wants to spend an equivalent amount for new technology, and there's only enough for one or the other, someone has to decide who's going to get it. That someone must be one of the people who create or execute the company's strategy.

How to Budget

The worst way to budget is to say, "Here's what we spent last year. Let's add 3 percent to each budget item."

Good managers demand zero-based budgeting, even though it's more time-consuming and demanding. In zero-based budgeting, you look closely at each item in the budget and ask, "What do we really need to spend to reach our objectives?"

To do this effectively requires two things: First, your boss has to give you guidelines. He or she should forecast revenues for the company or your unit and estimate what level of expenses are allowable based on the company's financial goals.

Best Tip

When creating a budget, scrutinize each category and ask, "What do I really need to spend here to get the job done?"

Frequently, this doesn't happen. Bosses sometimes ask you for figures so they can decide whether they work or not. This is, of course, doing the job backwards.

Second, you have to become intimately acquainted with your costs. Keep records on each item, so you can budget for it based on good assumptions. These records show, for instance, trends in pricing. That allows you to make good guesses.

Keep records that show what you spend in each category from year to year. It'll make budgeting far more pleasant.

Zero-based budgeting helps you manage better by cutting waste and looking for places to improve productivity. For example, say you have a budget line for temporary help. Your records detailing what you spent on temps helps you come up with a realistic figure for the coming quarter or year. But the line item should also give you pause: Did temps accomplish what you wanted? Did they require more supervision? Would it save money to hire a person permanently? Can you change operations to eliminate the need for temps? These are the kinds of questions a good budget analysis prompts.

A budget should also reflect reality. If you have the same figures for each item month in and month out, you've most likely averaged your yearly costs on a month-by-month basis. Build seasonal variations into the budget so it reflects reality.

Know Your Performance Indicators

You should also have a keen grasp of performance indicators for your specific work.

Briefly, you should know how much key transactions cost in your department or business. For example, if you are in charge of a customer service unit, know what the cost of each call is. That can be an aggregate amount, like $62 per call. Or it can be broken down—$3 for the telephone time, $7.50 for an employee's time, $18 for the information technology that permits you to respond quickly, etc.

When you know figures like this, you can budget based on anticipated volume.

Visit Your Budget Weekly

Consider charting your budget weekly rather than monthly. Sometimes a month is too long to make quick, necessary changes in direction.

Also, you can pretend your weekly budget is like an allowance. You know how much you have to spend, so you pick out the bills or make purchases for the services you absolutely need, leaving the less important items for next week.

Analyze Variances

Once you have real-world, accurate figures in place, track closely the difference between budgeted and actual spending. It's easy to set up a spreadsheet with spaces for your budget figure, actual spending, and the variance between the two:

	Current Period		
Account	**Actual**	**Budget**	**Variance**
Accounting	879.78	500.00	(379.78)
Blueprints	1,345.00	1,500.00	155.00
Depreciation	1,400.00	1,200.00	(200.00)
Dues	500.00	500.00	0.00
Entertainment	1,981.54	2,000.00	18.46
Gas	253.19	300.00	46.81
Janitorial	150.00	150.00	0.00
Licenses	1,500	0	(1,500.00)
Materials	14,395.62	12,500	(1,895.62)

An alternative is to have your computer whiz create a program that produces an "exception report." This report provides data only on the accounts that vary from budget outside a specific range. For example, if you're over budget on temp services by 2 percent, it wouldn't show up. But if you're over by 12 percent, it does. The exception report thus gives you time to act.

Question every variance, both positive and negative.

For example, you haven't spent as much as you thought for rent over the first six months? Why? Did you make a mistake? Did someone forget to pay or record a bill? Look into every variance until you're satisfied you've uncovered, and fixed, the cause. (Or until you decide you must crawl to your boss with a request to increase spending.)

In some industries with narrow profit margins, watching

*B*est *T*ip

Watching variances and acting on them may be the key to your success—or failure.

variances is absolutely essential to success. A contractor I know wins jobs based on excellent estimating. But if he doesn't complete the work on budget, he knows, he'll be out of the business in no time.

He constantly monitors the budget for each job. If there's even a minor variance, he jumps right on it. His margin is too thin to let it wait—if he does, it may be too late to do the job profitably.

Build in Productivity Gains

Some companies meet their numbers by building in productivity gains. You give managers progressively less money each year to do the same amount of work. It's up to them to come up with productivity improvements so they don't go over budget.

This method sounds draconian, but it's a good way to contain costs, and a good way for you to spot managerial skill.

Create a Market Economy Inside the Firm

To do a really good budgeting job, and to contain costs, you must know what each service or product you receive costs. That's easy to do when a vendor sends you a bill.

But what about when you "buy" an item inside the company? For example, you arrange for in-house designers to work on your new product idea. Or you call in human resources to find you a new secretary.

Quantify these costs, too. Each transaction should have a dollar value.

Cypress Semiconductor goes one step further: Its units actually exchange money in the fashion of a market economy. And they take another leap that promotes in-house efficiency. Units can shop outside the company for a better price. Cypress's fabrication plants compete with each other for work—as well as with Asian factories outside the company.

Without a system of quantifying internal costs, it's hard to figure the real cost of doing business.

How to Ask for More Money

The discussion so far assumes that business is stable, and your budgetary needs don't change much from one year to the next. That's rarely the case.

Sometimes you see an opportunity, and you need money to exploit it. Or, despite your best efforts, you're swamped with work and your operation is becoming inefficient. Then it's time to ask for more funds.

Many managers go about requesting funds the wrong way. They go to the boss and say, for example:

1. "I need the money to buy a machine and enhance quality."
2. "I need another person, otherwise we won't be able to meet our deadlines."
3. "We've got a good crew of people in this department. I'd like a 5 percent increase in payroll to raise salaries and make sure we keep them happy."

All these things sound good to most people. It's all for the good of the company. But these statements don't sound good to senior managers, whose job it is to create value for shareholders.

What senior managers want to hear is how you'll take company money and make it grow. If you put your requests in terms they understand, you'll often get your way. But you have to do your homework. Make proposals you are sure fit in with corporate strategy. And do detailed cost-benefit analyses.

Let's look at how the requests above for more money might be presented more effectively.

1. "The rejection rate for component X is one in one thousand, costing us about $28,000 a year. I've looked into purchasing a new precision planer with computer controls that will allow us to set tolerances to a millimeter. That will improve the rejection rate to one in ten thousand, which will bring the cost of rejections down to around $9,000 at current levels of output. The machine and controls cost $36,750, including training and downtime, making the payback period . . ."

Best Tip

When you ask for money, always show how the money is an investment that will have a good return.

2. "We've been having trouble meeting schedules lately. I've tried to fix the problem by doing [x, y, and z]. Nothing seems to work. Increasing overtime costs more and still takes care of only half the problem. Missing deadlines is costing us $4,350 a month. I propose we put a new technician on the job. It'll not only save us nearly $50,000 a year, but she can spend 10 percent of her time doing project proposals, meaning we'll be able to bid for more work. If we get 10 percent more work—all manageable with a new person—we'll increase sales to . . ."

3. "I fear we're not paying our key employees enough. Last month we lost another one to ACME. I sat down and figured what a new hire costs us in recruiting, training, and

productivity lost. It's around $13,000. Multiply that by the six people we've lost and we're talking $78,000 so far—and we've still got two months to go in the fiscal year. I had coffee the other day with Jack, who jumped over to Phillips. He was real nice and told me exactly why he left: money and benefits. The thing is, they are only paying him 7 percent more. I called Jackie, who went to ACME, and she told me she left for about the same amount. Both said they would have stayed if we'd been close—like 5 or 6 percent higher. So what I'd like to do is . . ."

You get the picture. Show how current practices are costing you money. Show in detail how spending money could more than offset those costs. Put it down on paper so people can see you've done your homework and you understand financial realities.

If you've analyzed the situation effectively, you'll often find your requests approved.

The Agile Manager's Checklist

✔ Take your company's financial goals. Set a budget that ensures you are doing your part to help reach them.
✔ Start afresh each year. Zero-base your budget.
✔ Analyze budget variances at least monthly.
✔ Understand that senior managers don't want to hear about expenses—they want to hear about investments.

Index